career highlights*:

- Performed a solo concert at The White House

- Awarded The 2008 ASCAP Morton Gould Young Composer of The Year Award for her original composition, "Northern Lights", Youngest award recipient ever.

- Appeared on The Ellen Degeneres Show 5 times

- Made her professional debut at The Ravinia Music Festival at the age of 5, Youngest performer in their 100 year history

- Performed at Ravinia for three consecutive summers

- Youngest student to attend The Aspen Music Festival & School

- Made her classical orchestral debut performing Mozart Piano Concerto No.23, K.488 with 2 major symphony orchestras

- Lent her performing talents to benefit many charities including: Children's Hospital of Los Angeles, The Noble Awards, Children's Hospital of Chicago, Susan G. Koman For a Cure, Ronald McDonald House and many more.

*as of the release of Always True CD - Nov 2009, Emily age 7

a musical scrapbook

Many people ask how Emily gets ideas to compose her original music. Inspiration comes to her in many ways. It could be from a book she is reading (Northern Lights), noticing something in nature (Snowdance, Aspen), a place she has visited (Ka'iulani, Wyndham Court), or a special occasion (Once Upon A Wish, Tomorrow's Wishes). Through her songs, Emily creates a musical scrapbook of her life. Songs come to her every day - she hears life in music and music in life.

a musical ambassador

Music is the true ambassador between people. It needs no common language - it is the language understood and felt by all. The response to Emily's music has been felt across the globe - from Malaysia to Norway, Australia to Argentina, Slovakia to Japan. The emotional response to her sounds are universal and it is a joy to feel the common ties that unite all of us through her music.

Tomorrow's Wishes

music by
Emily Bear

Gently ♩ = 96

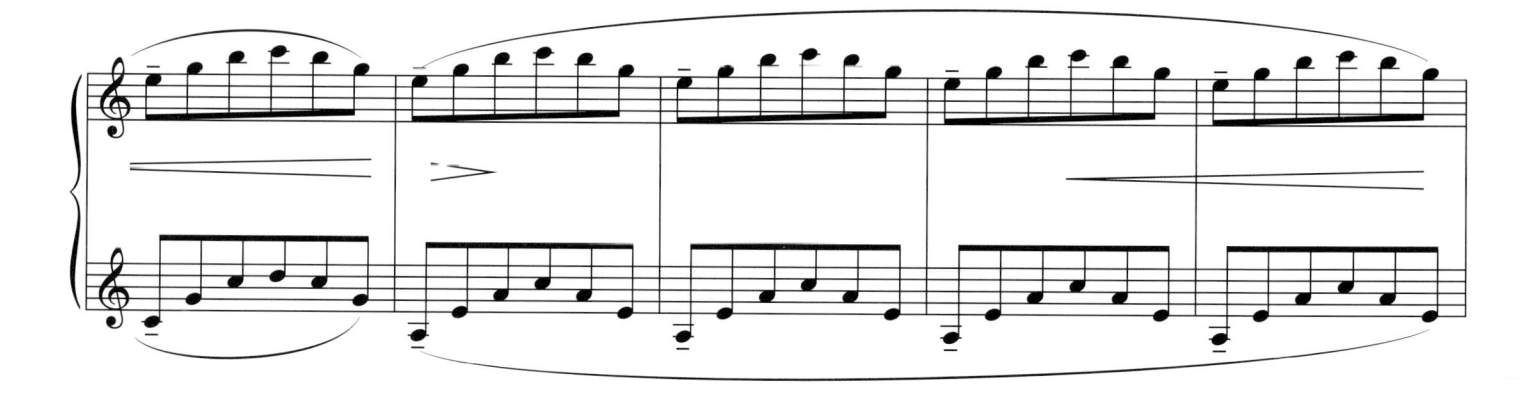

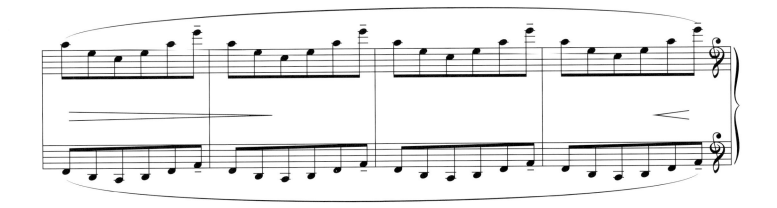

Tempo I

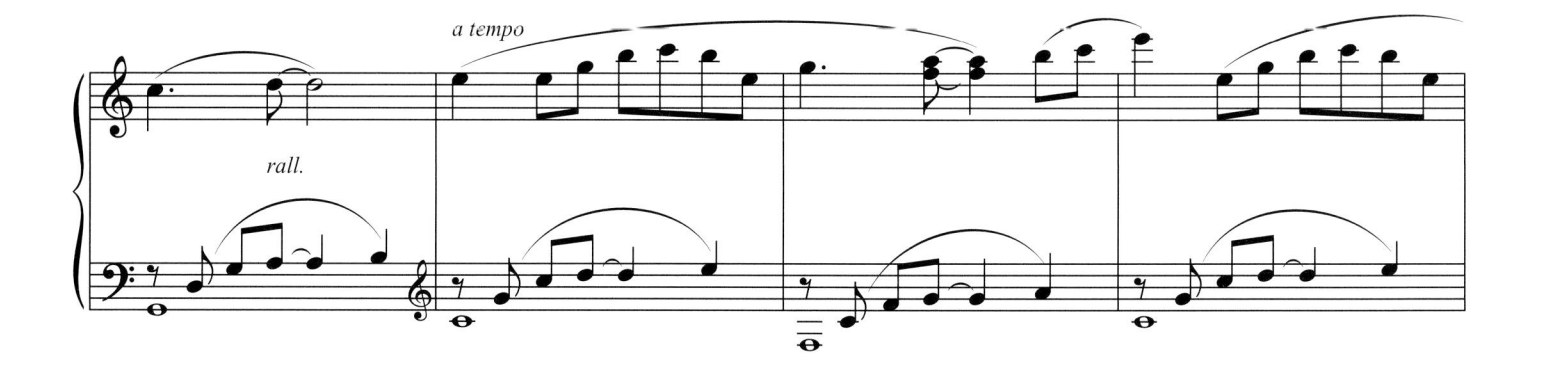

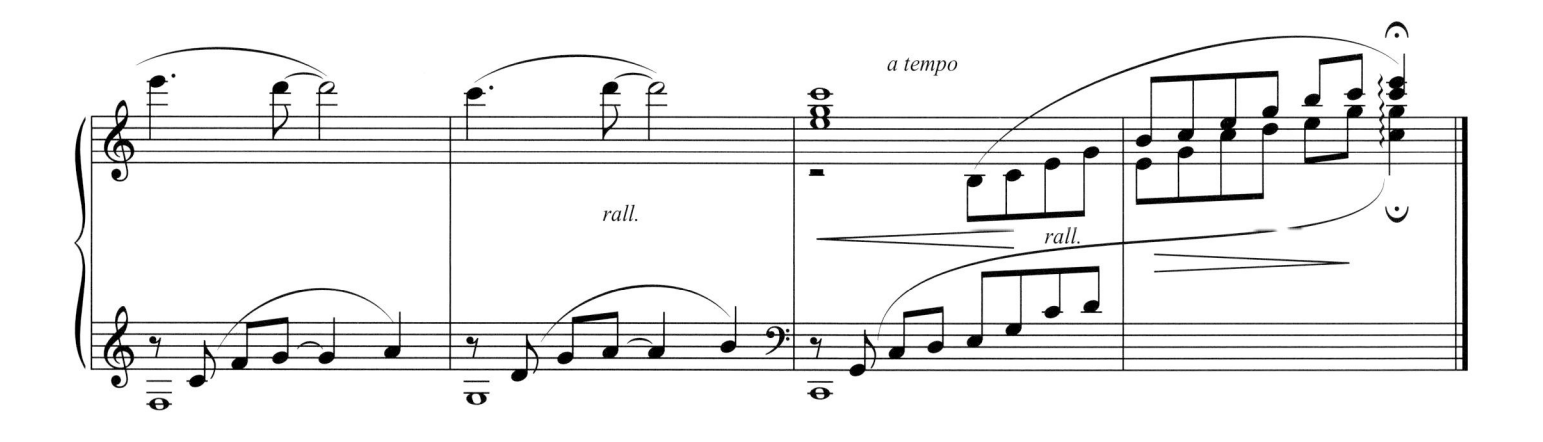

The Way Back To Love

music by
Emily Bear

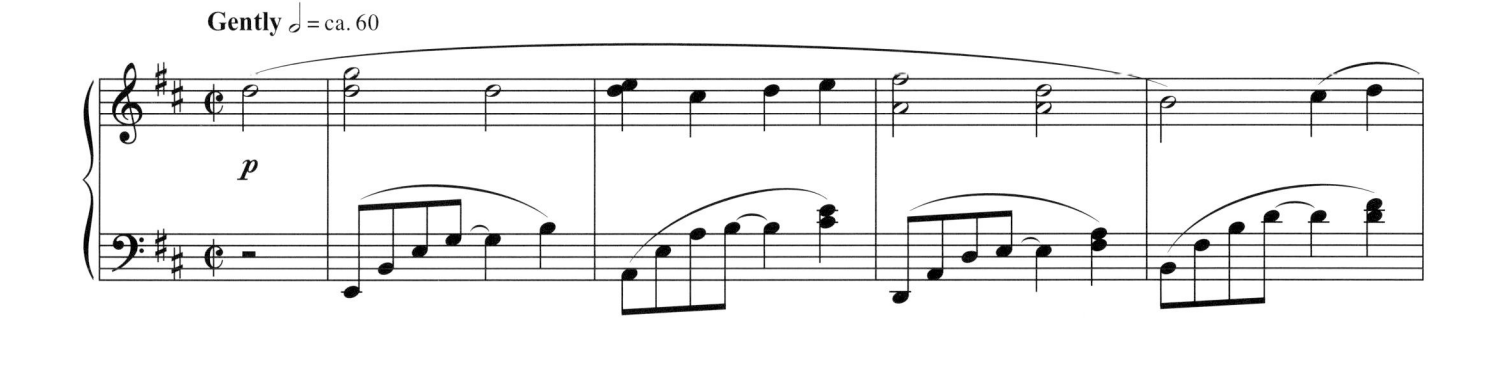

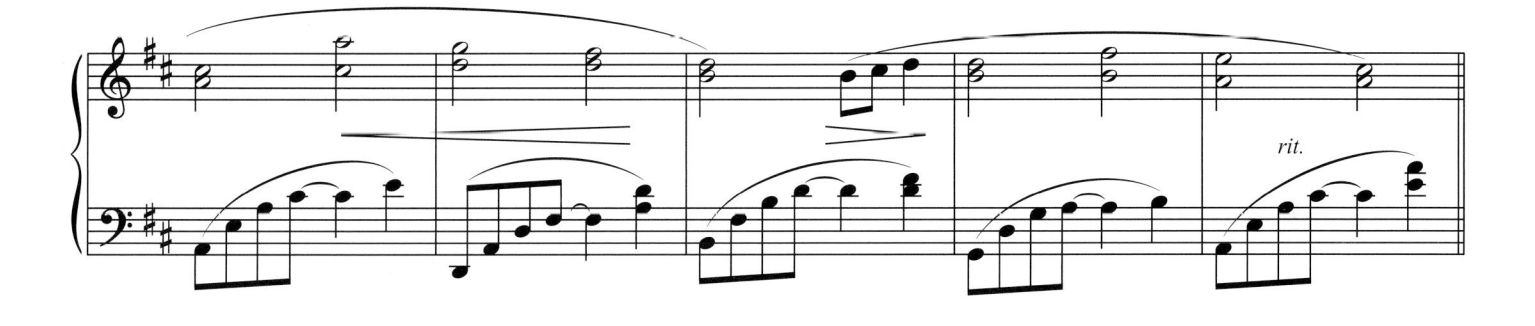

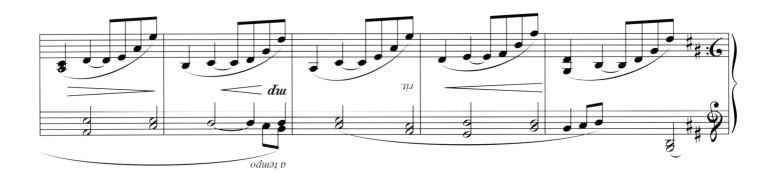

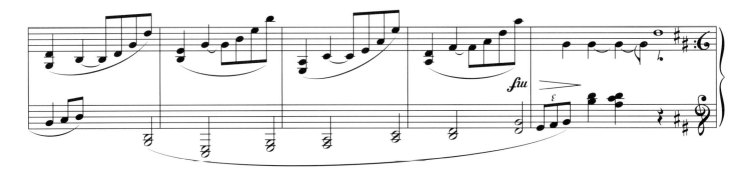

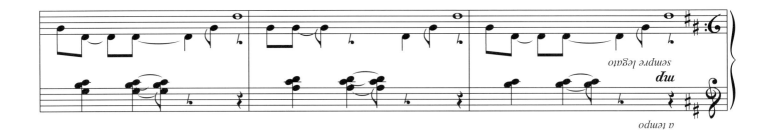

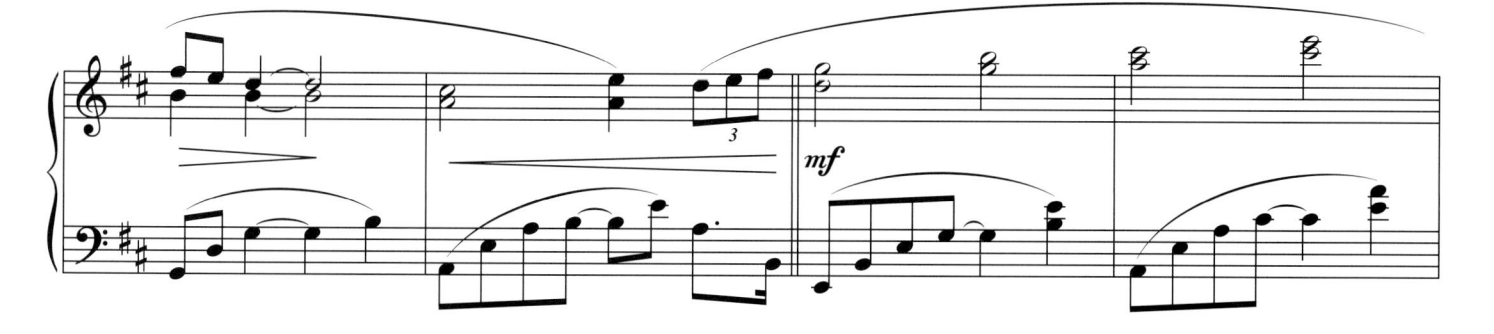

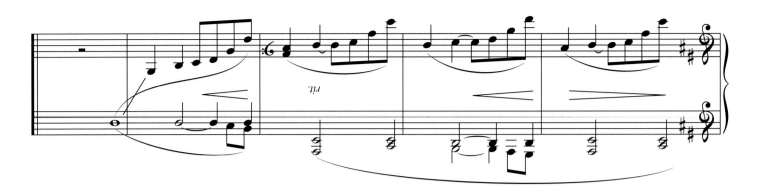

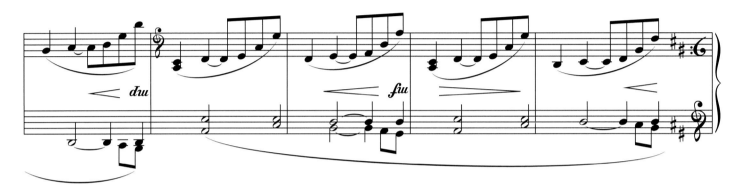

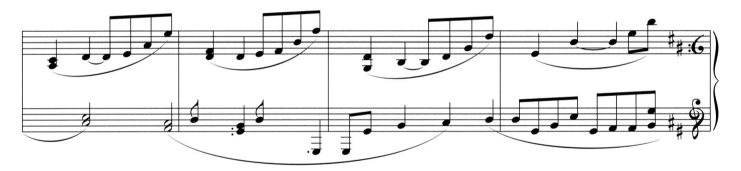

23 free

music by
Emily Bear

Moderato ♩ = ca. 112

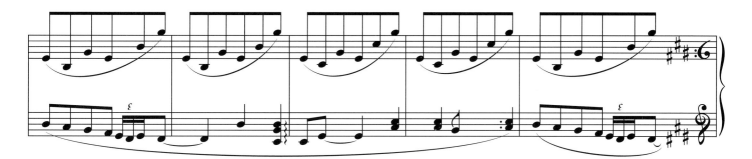

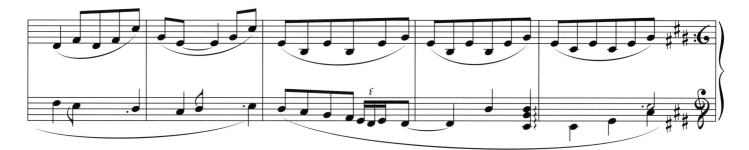

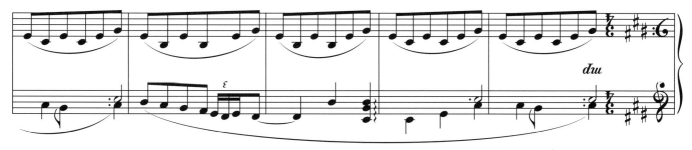

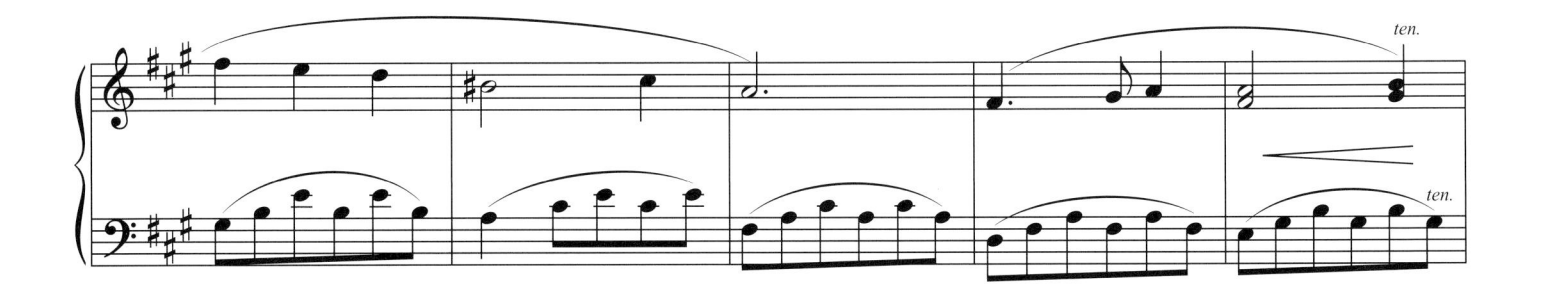

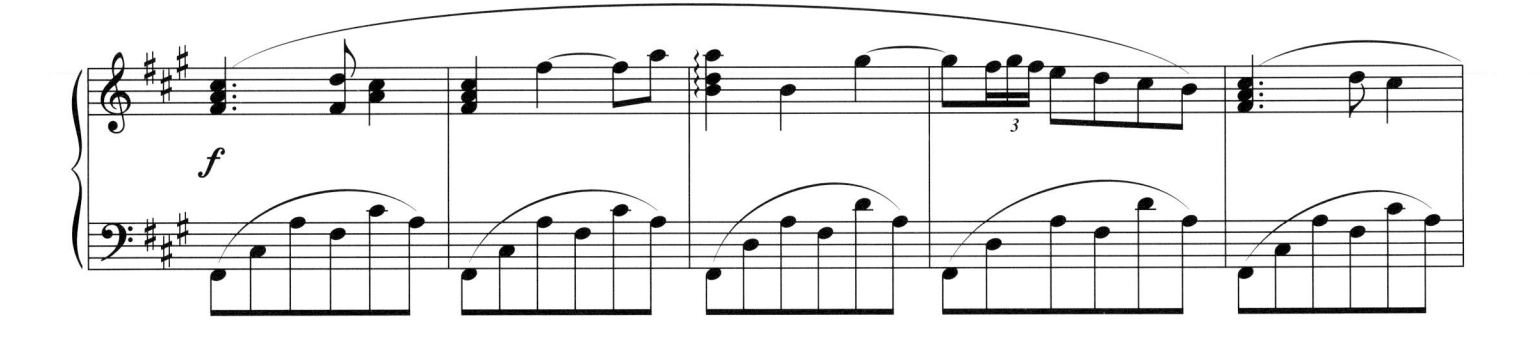

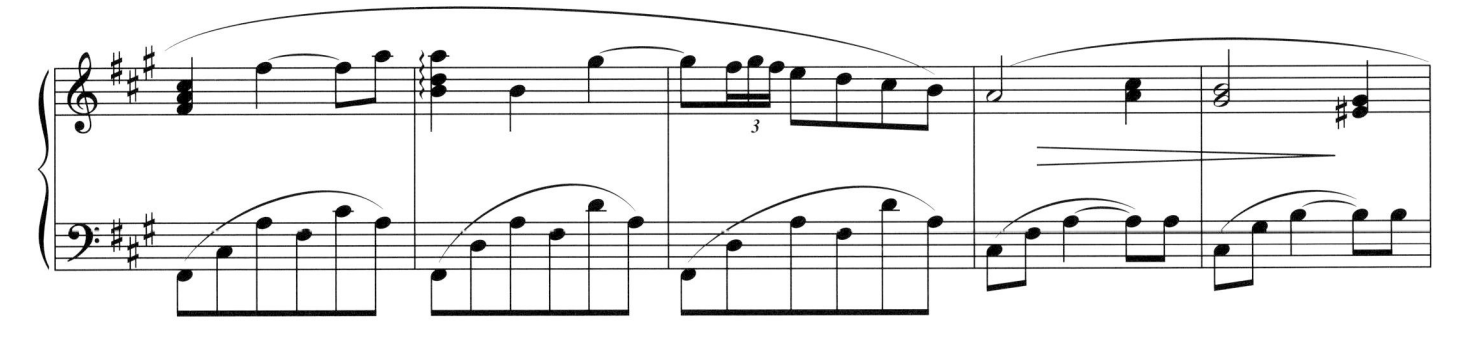

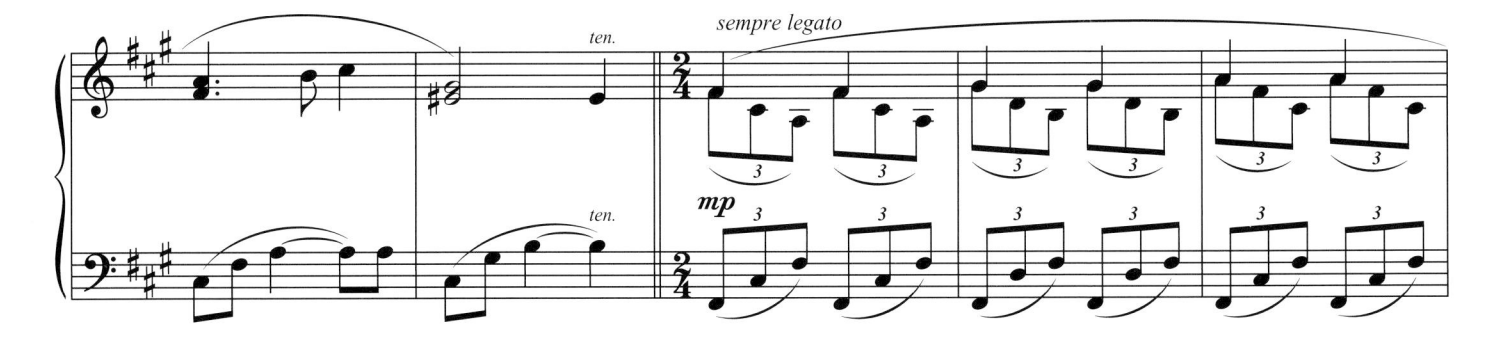

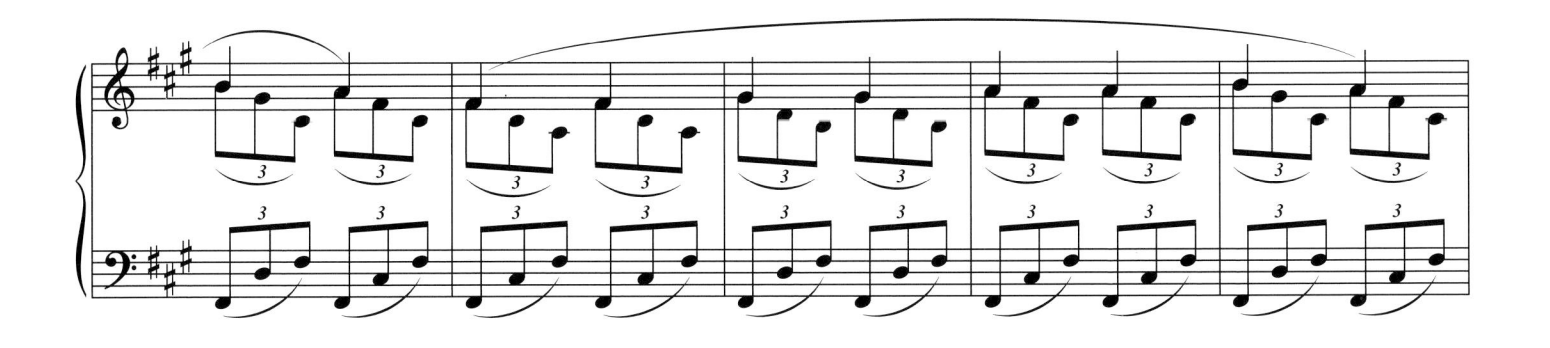

15

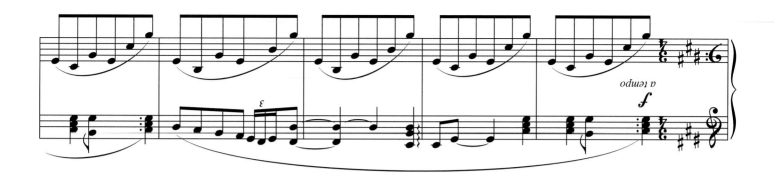

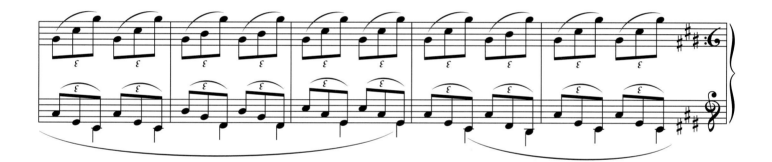

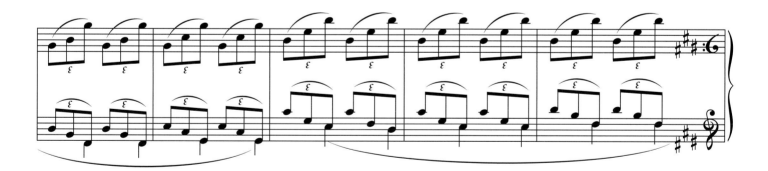

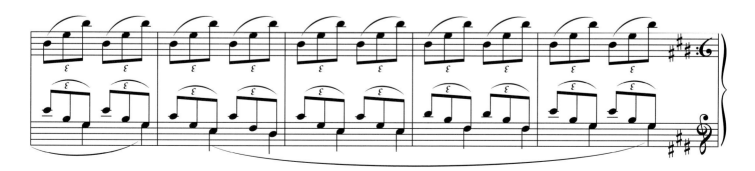

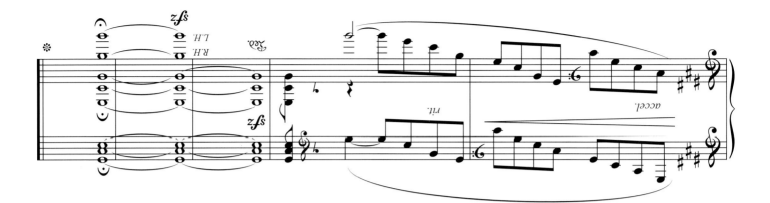

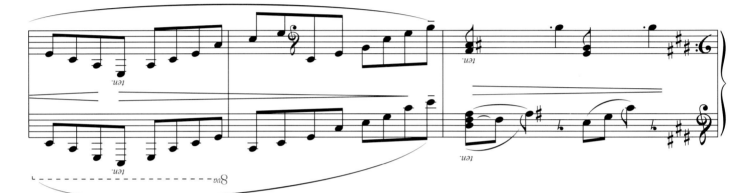

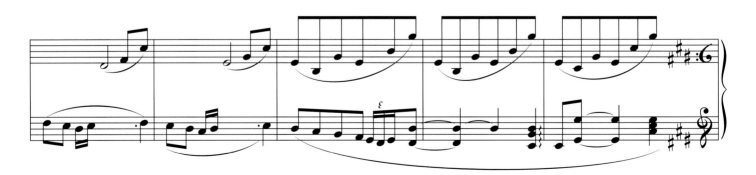

March Majestic

music by
Emily Bear

Tempo di marcia ♩ = ca. 120

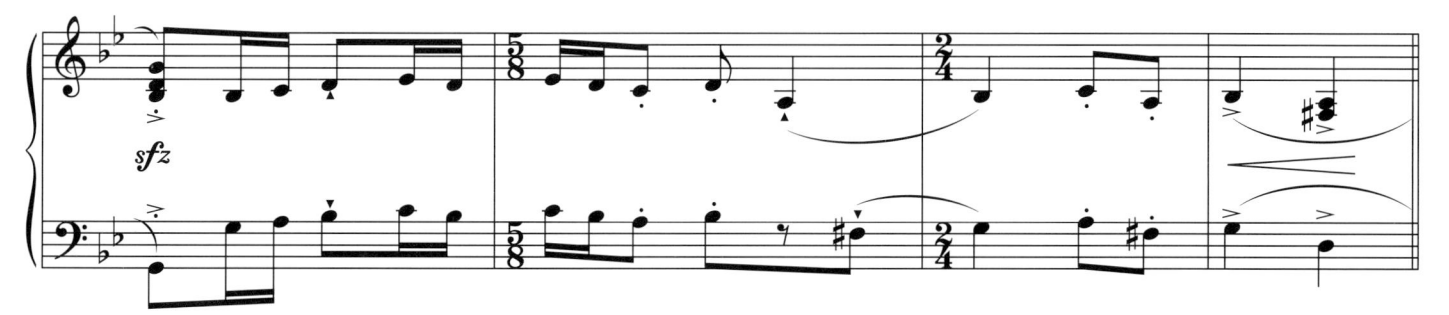

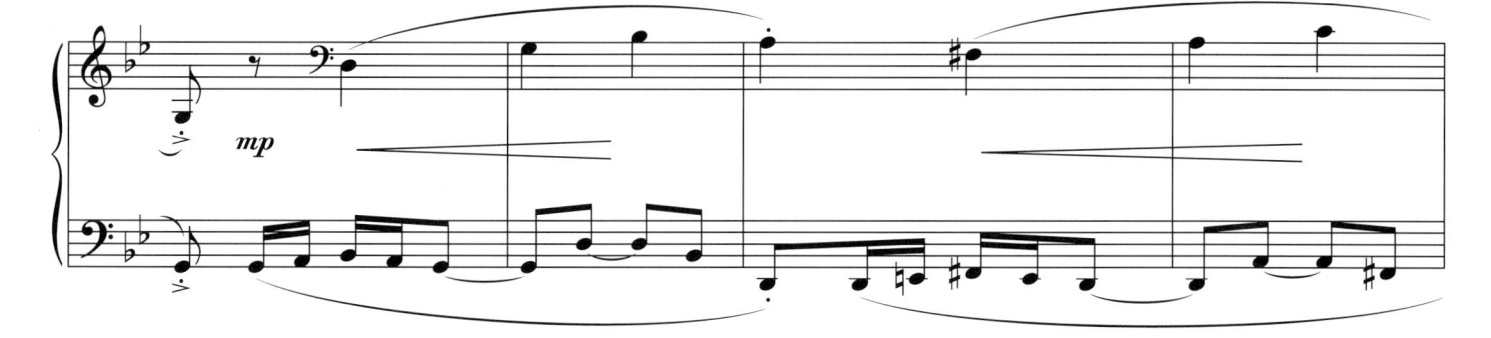

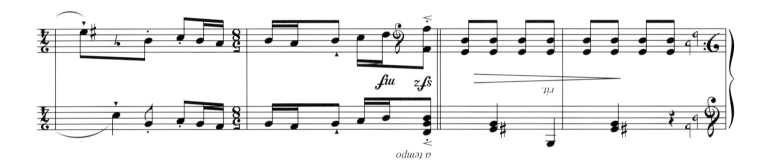

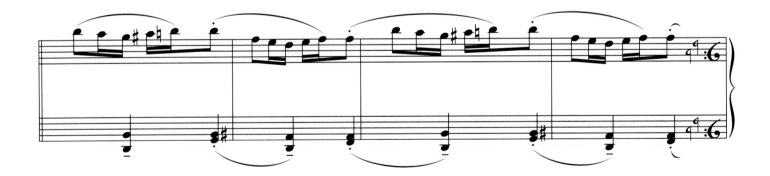

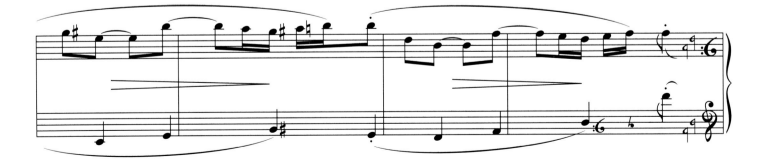

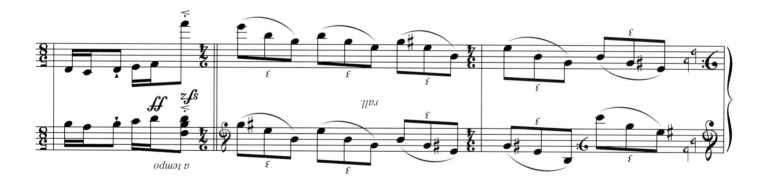

Indescribable

music by
Emily Bear

Gently, quasi rubato (♩ = ca. 80)

Flowing (♩. = ca. 60)

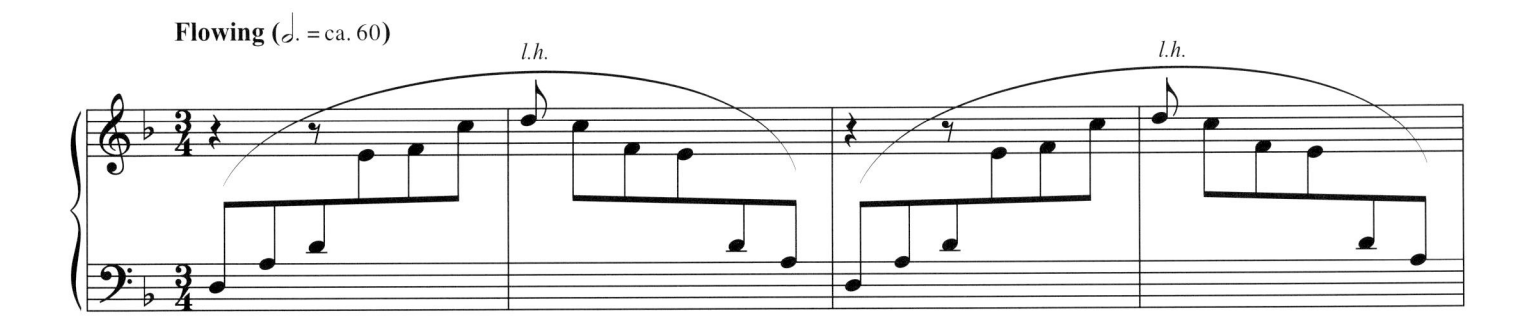

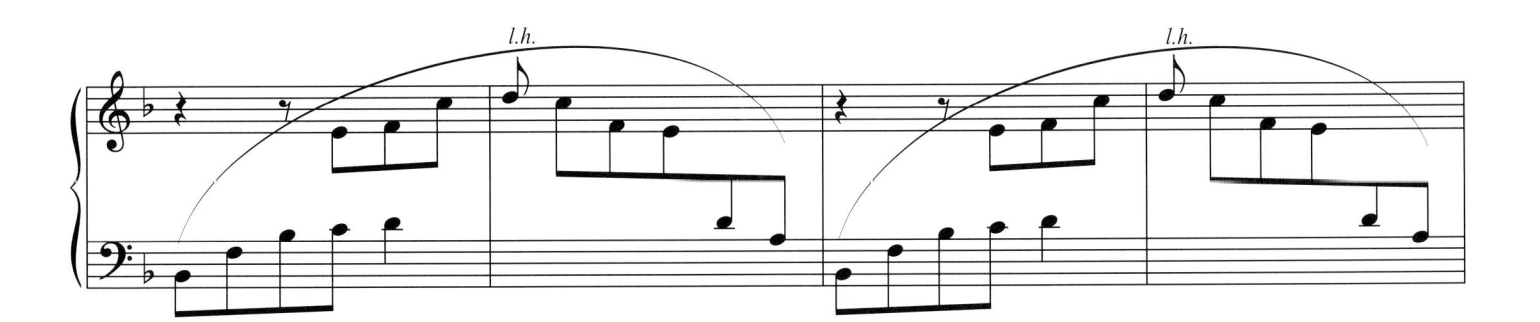

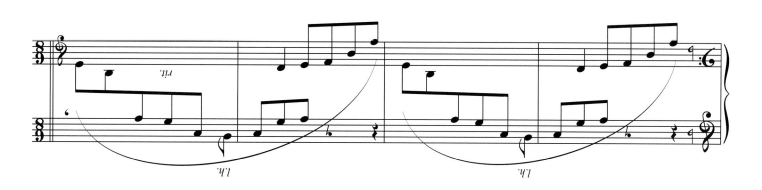

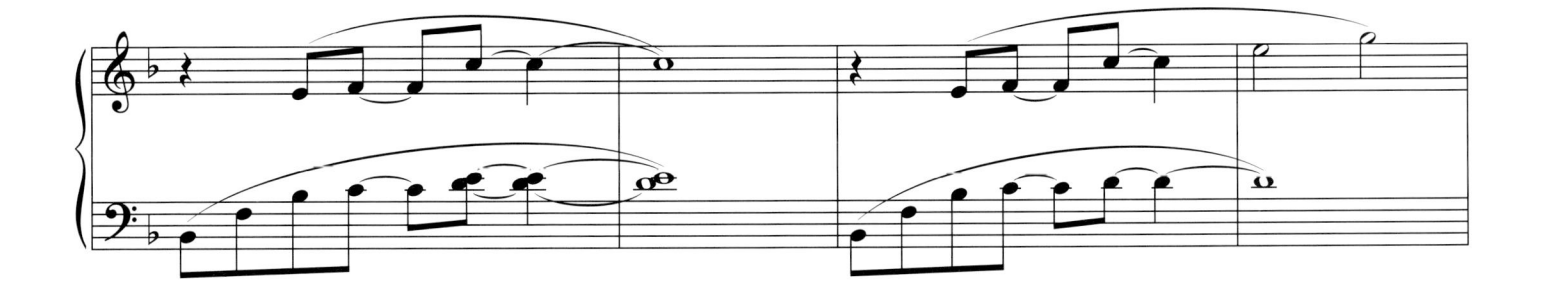

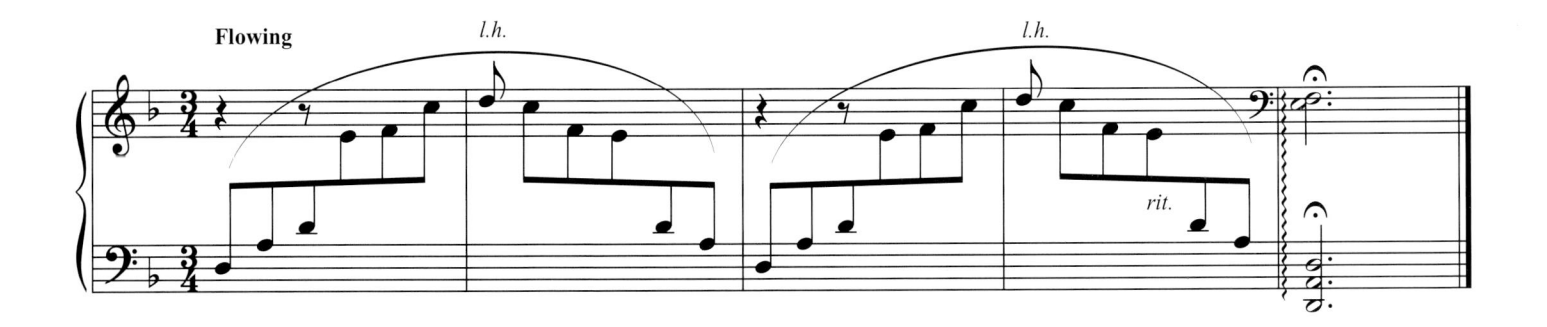

Jazz Angles

music by
Emily Bear

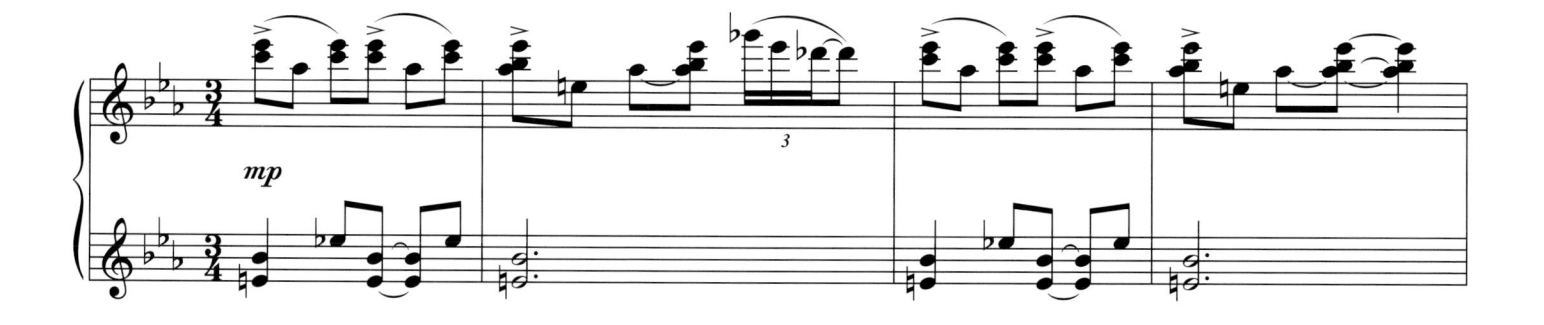

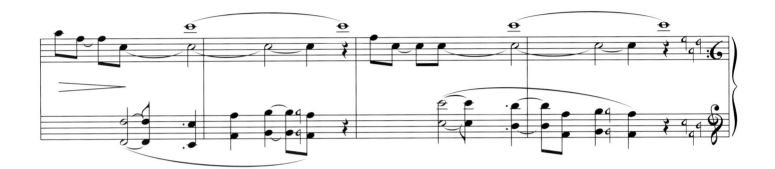
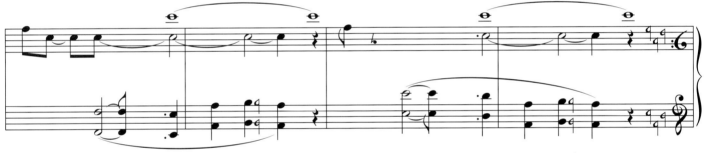
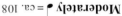

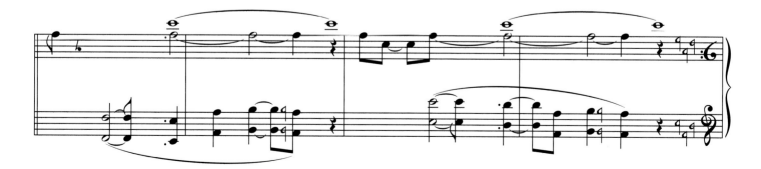

Ka'iulani

music by
Emily Bear

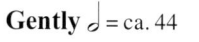 

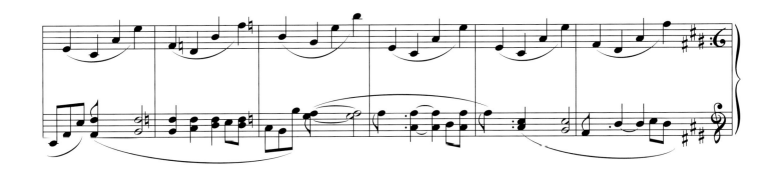

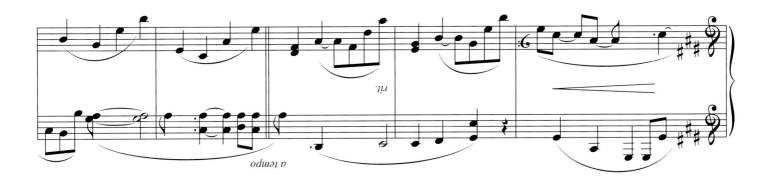

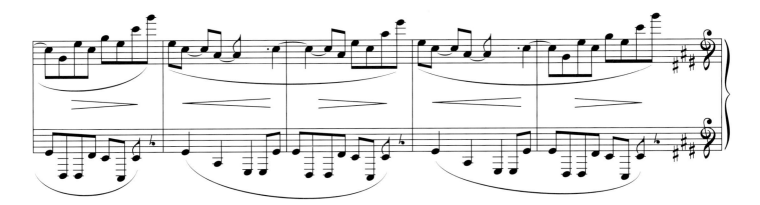

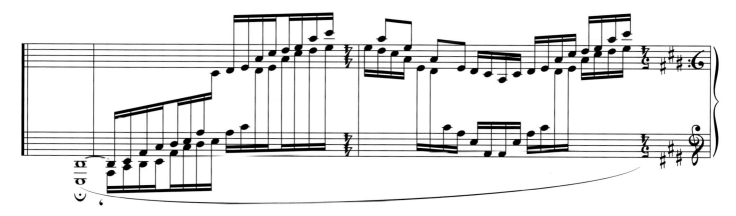

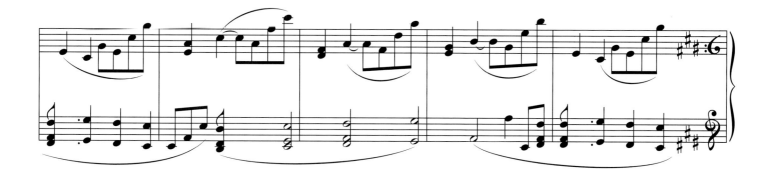

Joie

music by
Emily Bear

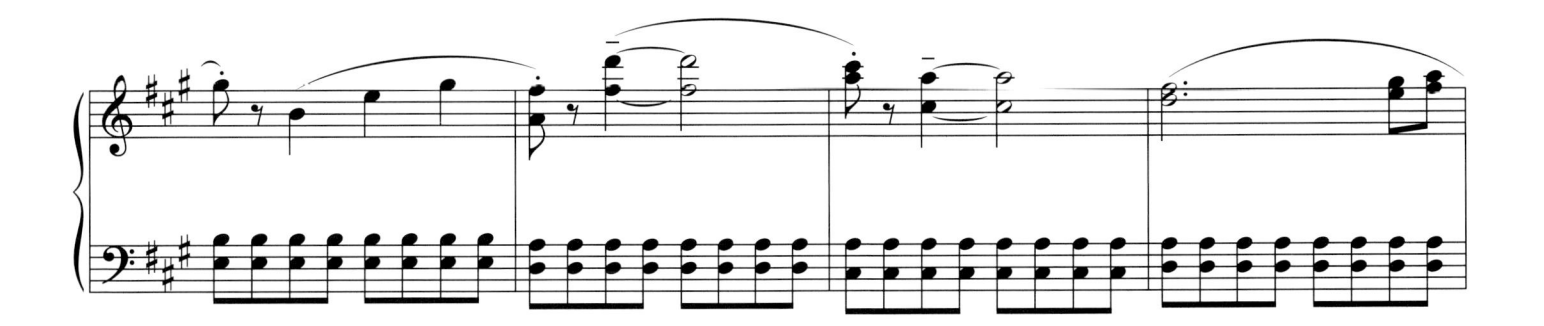

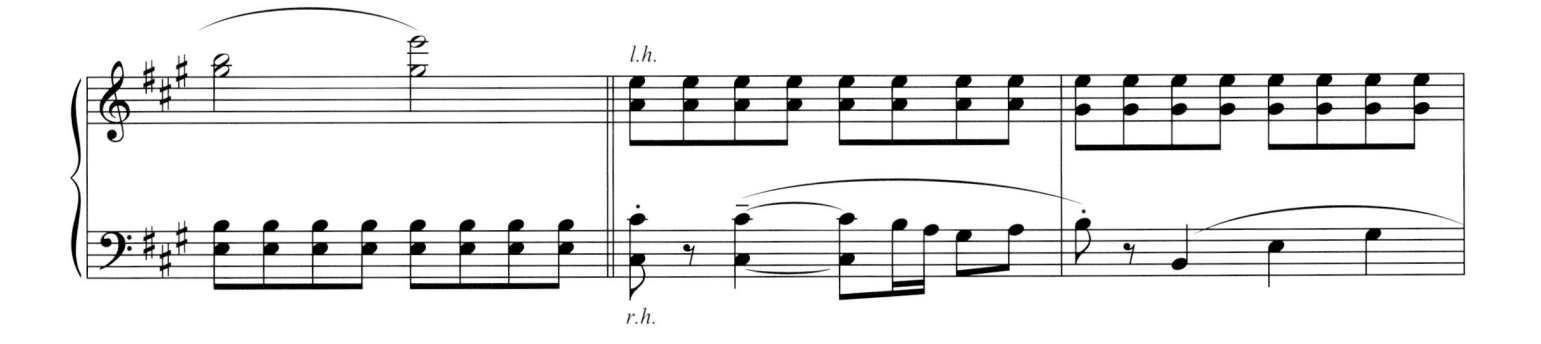

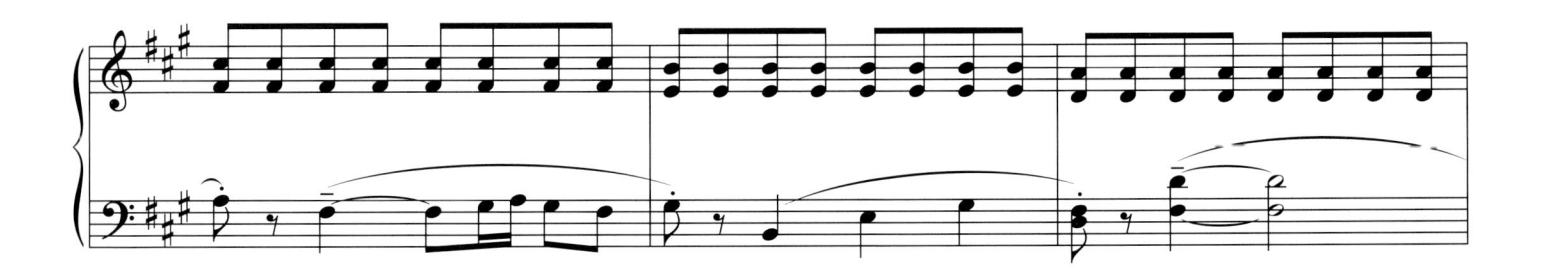

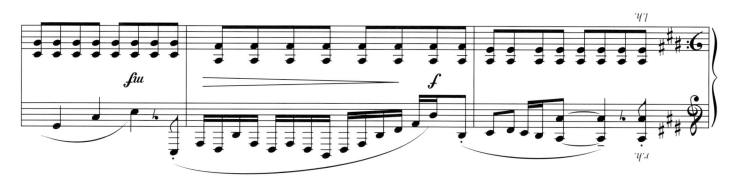

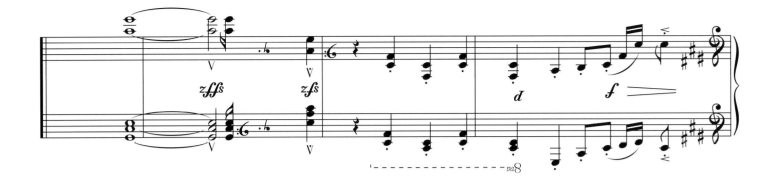

A New Day

music by
Emily Bear

Moderately ♩ = ca. 120

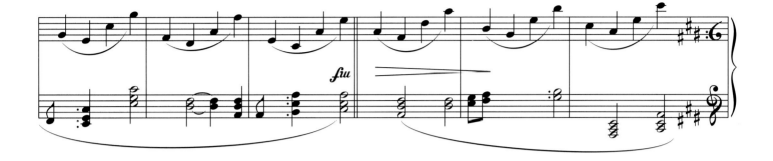

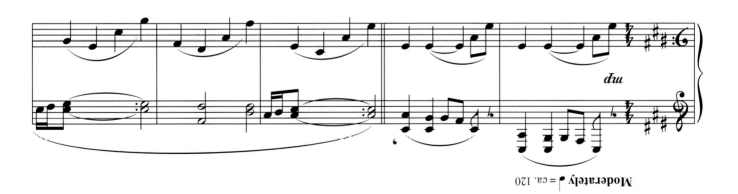

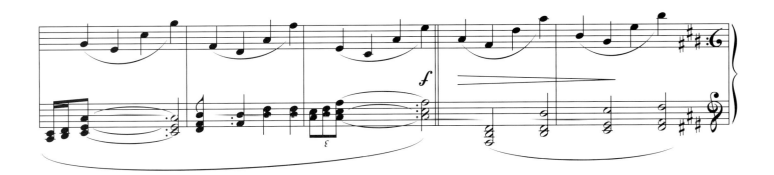

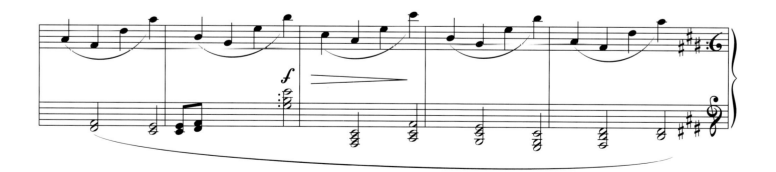

Always True
Piano Solo

music by
Emily Bear

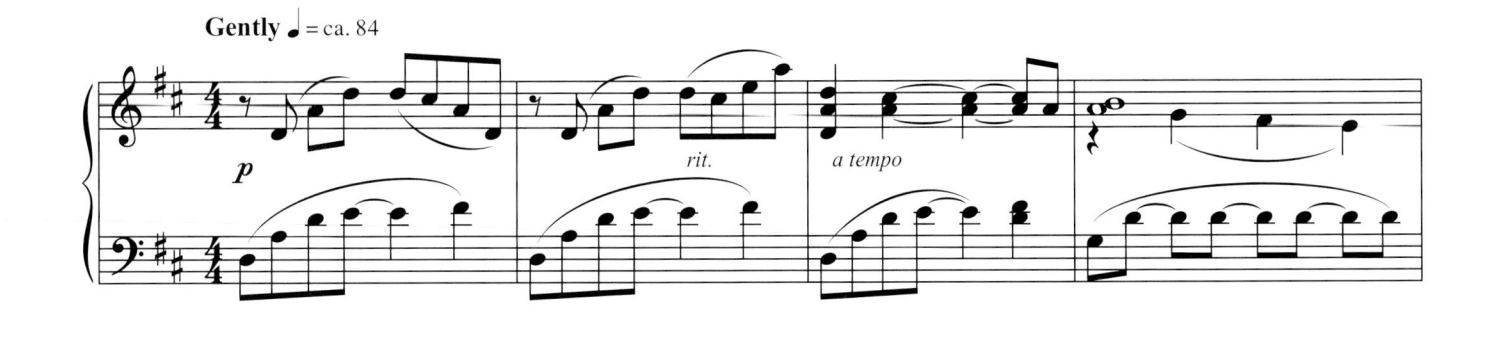

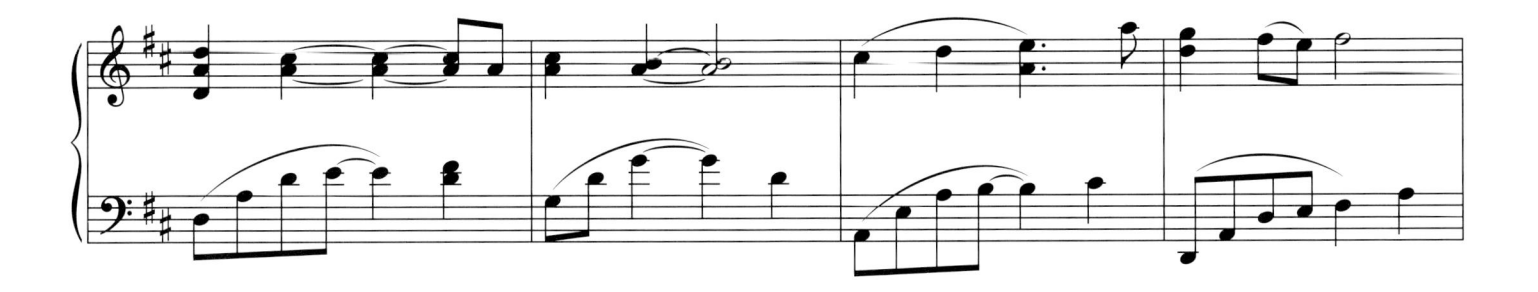

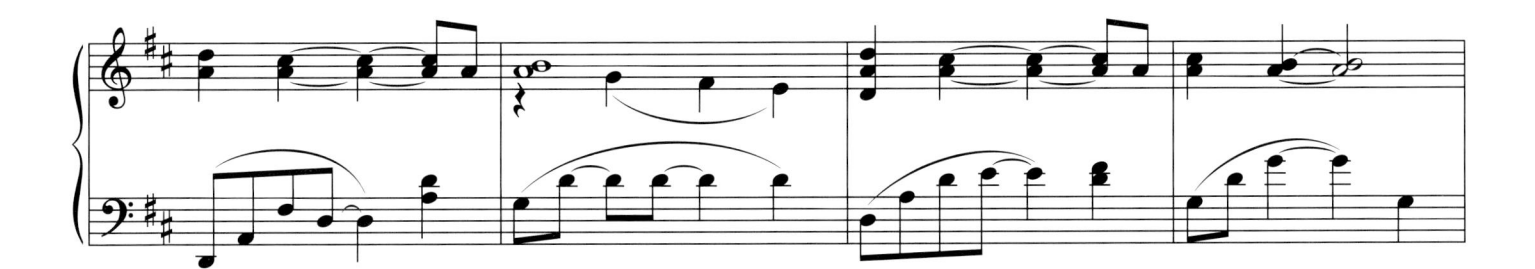

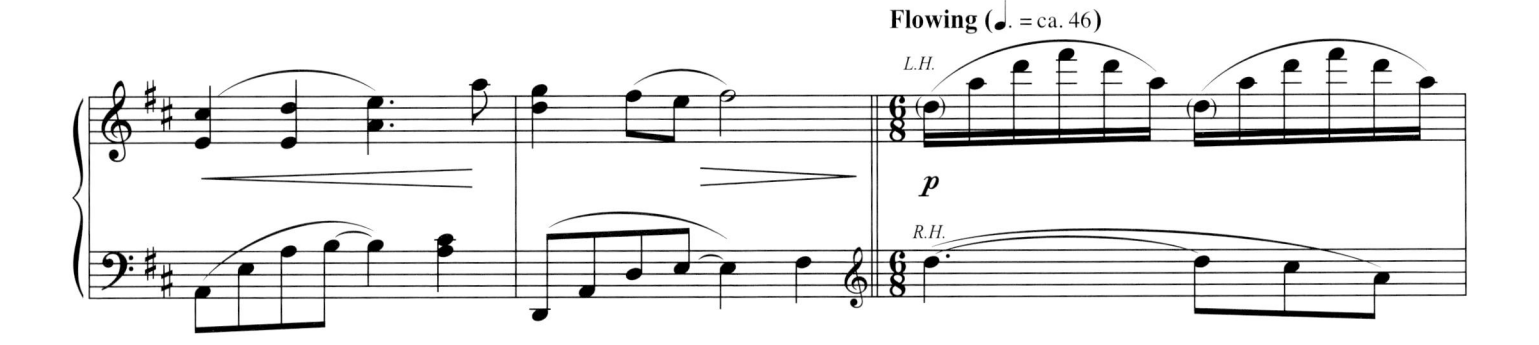

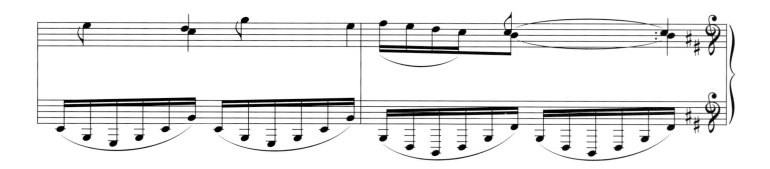

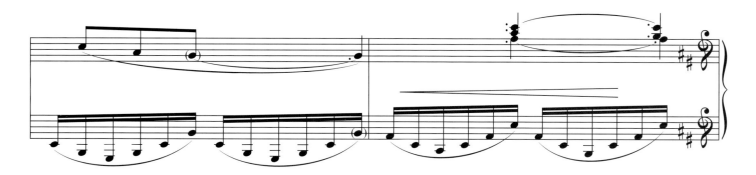

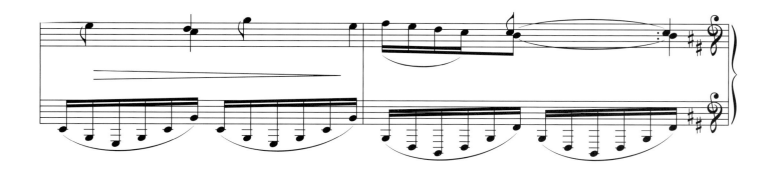

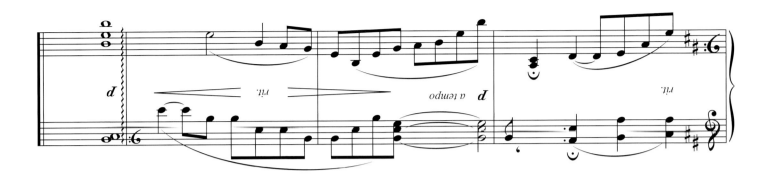

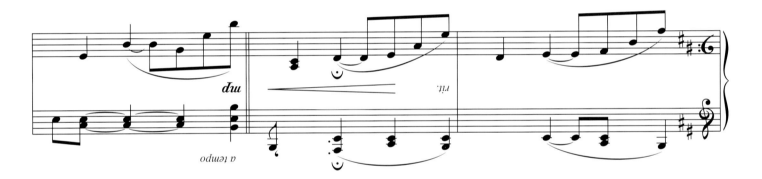

Always True
with vocals

lyrics by
Andrea Bear

music by
Emily Bear

nit - ing_____ our two hearts as one once a - gain.

Flowing ($\dot{\bullet}$. = ca. 46)

Male

I_____ see you there, stand-ing as if no time passed since

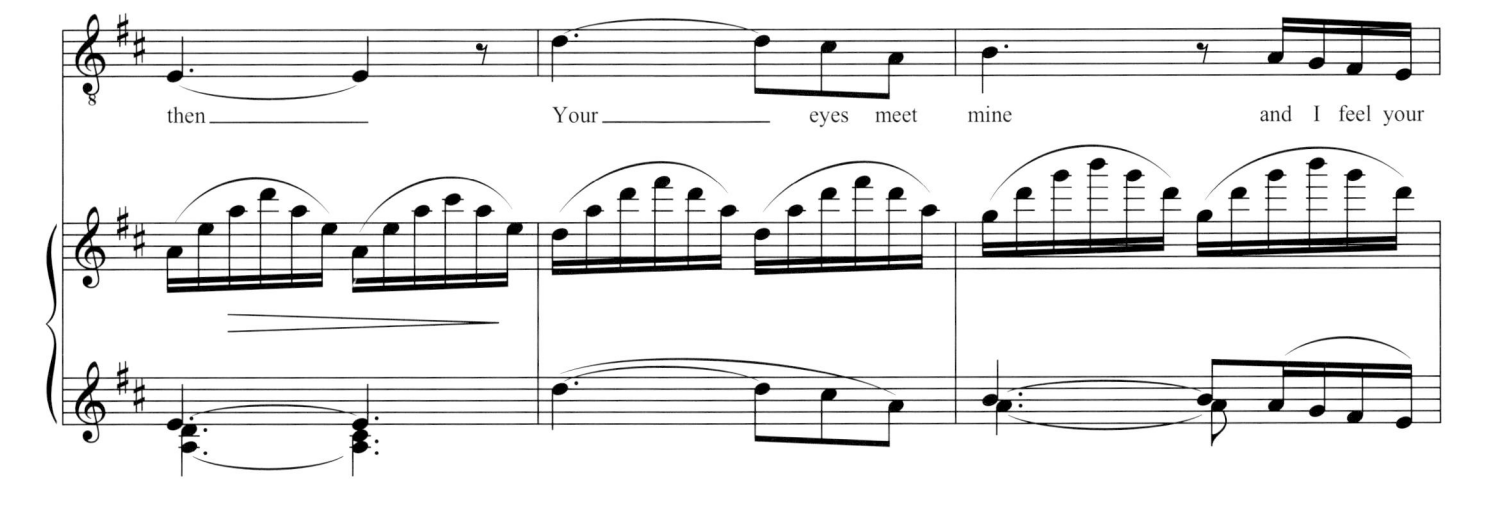

then_____ Your_____ eyes meet mine and I feel your

arms a - round me then._____

rit.

43

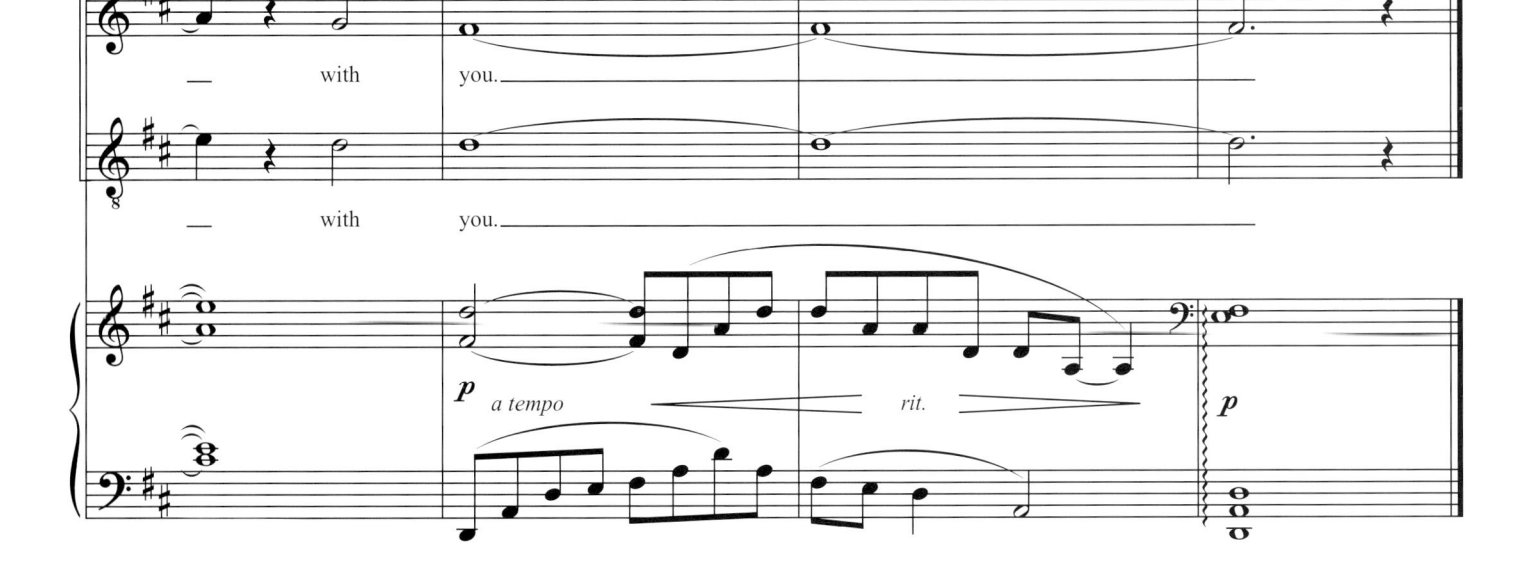

always true

I look at you
feelings surround us
bringing us together again

I reach for you
hands touch, uniting
our two hearts as one
once again

> I see you there
> standing as if no time passed since then.
> Your eyes meet mine
> And I feel your arms around me then.

> I missed you so
I missed you
> Seeing you heals me
Heals us

Bringing us together again
And now I …
> *…and when I look at you*
And when your eyes meet mine
Then I know…

I will be always yours
Now 'til the end of time
Always true
> - with you

I love you so
> I missed you
Be here for always
> always

Always true
With you

Book Design by:
Bill Edmundson & Andrea Bear
Photos by:
Andrea Bear
www.emilybear.com

emily bear

always true

Jordan King Music USA

P.O. Box 271, Rockford, IL 61105

ISBN: 978-0-9826015-2-5